PRAISE FOR DANIEL KNAUF

"Written as a soul song for longing, Knauf's collection is both a dream and an awakening."

— STEPHANIE M. WYTOVICH, BRAM STOKER
AWARD-WINNING AUTHOR OF BROTHEL

"In Daniel Knauf's two-part composition of poetry, the first passage is a kaleidoscope of the landlocked in endless roles, trying to believe in true love/magic while submerged in self-destruction & redemption. The coda is more than curious, it's an adrenaline rush, a noir dance of the impossible, delivered straight-up in a splintered glass."

— LINDA D. ADDISON, HWA LIFETIME
ACHIEVEMENT AWARD WINNER

"Knauf's poetry is cinematic, creating vast landscapes and scenes, on bridges, between land and sky. The multitude of characters create a rich, nonlinear story that mimics our memories, and our moments, and intertwines various worlds and moods, from all-consuming love, loneliness, superheroes, mythology, texting, technology, and Dante. Knauf is both direct and also strangely surreal."

— -JOANNA C. VALENTE, AUTHOR OF SEXTING
GHOSTS

T0145500

NOHO GLOAMING

& The Curious Coda of Anthony Santos

DANIEL KNAUF

CLⴝSH

Copyright © 2018 by Daniel Knauf

Cover by Matthew Revert

ISBN: 978-1-944866-20-4

CLASH Books

PO BOX 487 Claremont, NH 03743

All rights reserved.

No part of this book may be reproduced in any form or by any electronic or mechanical means, including information storage and retrieval systems, without written permission from the author, except for the use of brief quotations in a book review.

This book is a work of fiction. Names, characters, businesses, places, incidents and events are either the products of the author's imagination or used in a fictitious manner. Any resemblance to actual persons, living or dead, or actual events is purely coincidental.

CONTENTS

FOREWORD

"Fairy tales do not tell children the dragons exist. Children already know that dragons exist. Fairy tales tell children the dragons can be slain."

~ G.K. Chesterton

The following collection is of two minds, two intents.

The first, *NoHo Gloaming*, is a document of a personal journey composed over the three years following the end of my marriage. It was a confusing time. I felt isolated from my heart; so deeply cocooned in scar tissue that I wondered if I was capable of ever again experiencing joy or even sorrow. Indeed, as a dramatist, this spiritual paralysis threatened my very livelihood. How could I possibly write a convincing scene if I was incapable of tapping into its associated emotions from within my own story~well?

The heart, however, is a tough and resilient muscle.

Over those three years, I met a succession of extraordinary people, and with each relationship experienced the broad range of human emotions, from moments of transcendent ecstasy to protracted weeks of despair. Each relationship helped me discern my own faults and come to terms with long-held misconceptions I'd had about the nature of love and commitment.

Specifically, that in order to love and respect another, one must first learn to love and respect one's self.

Unlike my film and television work, which is created for a mass audience, *NOHO GLOAMING* was not composed with any audience whatsoever in mind—only for myself as a means of irrigating infected wounds in the only way I knew, through the writing process. As such, it represents the deepest, most closely guarded elements of myself.

Nevertheless, *NoHo Gloaming* is not a memoir. Though inspired by real people and actual incidents, the work should not be considered as sworn testaments of fact, but amalgams of disparate moments and various individuals.

Like all fiction, they are lies that tell the truth.

The second part of the collection, *The Curious Coda Of Anthony Santos*, a tale spun not to exorcize demons, but to throw on some loud dance music, get down and boogie with the bastards.

Written during a period of total isolation in Joshua Tree National Park during my 2016 hiatus from THE BLACKLIST, the coda is a ripping yarn inspired by classic pulp fiction, drawing on my earliest, most beloved influences, Poe, Lovecraft, Robert Bloch, Richard Matheson and Harlan Ellison—that streetwise gang of brilliant, bold, instinctive storytellers who pounded out work on rolls of butcher-paper for a nickel a word.

It is said that Li Po, the 8th Century Chinese poet, would write poems on rice paper, fold them into origami boats and launch them down the river to be lost or read by strangers. I always loved the purity of his process; poetry composed not for an audience, but for its own sake. Inspired by the master, I posted these poems as Status Updates on Facebook, taking quiet satisfaction as I watched each of them gradually descend into the data-pile; the 21st Century digital equivalents to Li Po's tiny origami vessels.

What I didn't know was there was a watchful recipient downstream, intercepting each bobbing craft, gingerly unfolding it, reading the words and spreading them on a shelf to dry in the sunlight. Though I composed the poems, Tina Ayres is the wonderful editor responsible for preserving them.

So if any credit is due for this collection, it should be directed to her.

- Daniel Knauf, Los Angeles, 2016

EDITOR'S NOTE

When I first discovered the lushly creative work of Daniel Knauf through the series *Carnivàle* I was reminded of the importance of the power held in all things creative. Possessing a gift to create worlds with words Knauf brings some much needed escapism to the masses in a way distinctly his own. The gritty honesty found in stylishly dark story lines and characters bursting with personality were all enthralling leading to me wonder what the mind behind them was like, and thus into contact with Daniel. The interview that followed offered readers a further glimpse into thoughts of the man who entertains the world with his words and led to my introduction to the various poems found in this compilation. His work often dark, and always genuine, is also a tribute to the weird, the outcast, and those down on their luck. These poems are no exception. Speaking of longing and loss and times often dark they convey an underlying feeling of hope, determination, and strength of will in a way that stirs emotions and seduces the senses leaving the readers wanting more.

- Tina Faye Ayres, *The Original Van Gogh's Ear Anthology*

NOHO
GLOAMING

BABY WEARS WAYFARERS

Nothing but dirt out here
Cracked dry roads and Dairy Queens
And half-naked trees
And church bells
And cows, lots of cows
And hash browns
And hair-dos
And men who drive rigs
And their women
Who best not ask why
Who best have dinner on the table
Who best fix their eyes forward
Always forward, never back

Landlocked.

California perched
On the bridge of her nose
The scent of salt, the cry of gulls
The endless heaving blue blue blue
Hidden behind Black glass.

29 PALMS

Wind today
out of the Southwest.
Steady.
Fat billows of sand rolling
between me and the mountains.
The horizon is a blur
between white and blue.

I am a bandit,
A dime-store Laurence of Arabia.
In my Ray Ban Wayfarers,
Docs,
Mad Max jacket,
Mouth and nose shrouded,
In a shemagh.
My Beretta strapped to my hip.
Powdered head-to-toe
With a fine patina
Of glittering brown dust.

If only I had a dirt-bike,
I would be a demigod.

HAIKU #1

Orpheus trembles
As soft footfalls of Maenads
Gather around him

ALICE

Sits on the dusty floor of the attic
White tights and pink gingham Sunday dress collecting grime.
Resting on her hip
Before a trunk of dolls.

She hums a tuneless tune
As she plays with one
Then the next
Then the next
Then the next.
And she tells each
And every doll.

"I love you most of all."

SLIPPING

under cool crisp sheets.
The scent of church incense.
A child's song muted behind a closed door.
The tug of a trout taking a baited hook.
A cryptic smile.
Hot strong coffee on a gray morning.
Kites dancing in a cloudless blue sky.
Chirping crickets.
Giggles and small bare feet hammering down a hallway.
Wind rustling tree leaves.
These moments
Seized and clenched
Like dry blades of grass
As we slide
Down
An ever-steepening
Slope.

Hello.

Goodbye.

TO DOROTHY

My father speaks to me
I can see his face
Hear his voice
Like wind teasing the reed on a clarinet
I knew him well
I remember him
But you
Your face
Your voice
I cannot conjure you at will
As I do with him
I used to wonder if it was
Because I was closer
To him
Until I realized
That a body cannot see the ocean
If it is submerged.

A CHILD

Hurtles down the hard, shiny sand
As the sea recedes, then
Squeals, pivots and runs like mad,
Giggling,
Away from the pounding surf
To be scooped up
By her mother
Sleek and laughing.
The woman looks at me
To make sure I didn't miss
This humble wonder
As unmistakable
As the Maker's thumbprint.

The child's sister
And I
Watch from a towel.
Smiling.
The sandcastle before us
Still lacks spires
And shells,
And seaweed pennants.
I ask the girl.

"Would you like to learn
How to catch sand crabs?"
She looks at me,
Yellow plastic spade
In hand,
And says,

"Yes."

BITS AND PIECES

Flotsam and
jetsam, smithereens and
debris. Photos that had been handled and bent
and scratched and wept upon. The scent
of brimstone and roses on a faded
tea-stained ribbon.

A fragment of a poem torn from a book.
A CD with a list of songs, the soundtrack to
a movie that is her, held
together with scotch tape and glue, misaligned and
torn sprockets that can only be run
once
through a projector before it
f-
f-
f-
flutters and
sticks and bubbles and burns.

You are left with a
bright
white

luminous square
on the screen.
The tick tick tick tick tick of a spinning reel.
And the last image
branded on your retinas:
a beautiful girl with a terrible scar,
visible only when you

blink.

UH-OH

We lean against my Ford
Side by side
Smoking cigarettes
Under a blood moon
I put my arm around her
Pull her close
She rests her head on my shoulder
We stand that way for a time
Soaking up silence.
I've known her for seven-and-a-half hours
And it already feels like
Forever

She says, "Everything's gonna be all right."

I say, "I know."

I FELL

The first time we met
She told me about the others
And I knew
She'd never been
With a man
Like me.

It never occurred to me
That she had no interest
In being with a man
Like me.

If you can't see the mountain
You're looking out
The wrong
Window.

THE FLASH IN LOVE

I am the Crimson Comet
The Scarlet Speedster
I can run at velocities
Incomprehensible
Immeasurable by any device
I can vibrate my molecules
And quantum tunnel
Through solid mass
Dimensions
Time
So fast am I
My touch
Imbues other creatures
With my power of acceleration.

And though I may appear
A braggart here
I am simply conveying
My stats
I am typically self-effacing
And kind to a fault
In fact
Over the years

To spare his feelings
I allowed the Man of Steel to tie me
Twice
Before I handed him
His ass
In a foot race.

And so you can only imagine
My astonishment
When she effortlessly passed me
Dancing silly circles around me
Giggling
At a pace
Incomprehensible
Immeasurable by any device
She ran ahead
Backwards
Facing me
A crooked grin on her lips
And said,

"Catch me if you can."

MAJESTIC

Post-modern digital Papa and Gertrude,
reduced
to texting brief salutations
between Bacchanalia. The feast
moving at the speed of light.

She throws her head back
and laughs. I discern
the girl who became
the woman...

OH MISSISSIPPI

A serpentine path of glittering stars
Meandering ceaselessly through black lands
Under a riot
Of a million billion distant dying suns
She is defined
Not by the darkness that hugs her banks
But the gorgeous motes of fire
Quivering in
Her current

A reflection of the Heavens?
No.
The Heavens
Reflect
Her.

I DOVE

A submerged caldera
Off the coast of a Pacific atoll
Crystal blue green
Teeming with life
And pulsing
Deep
Deep
Deep
In the fathomless dark
The promise of fire

Her eyes

This one
Puts down roots
To the core of the earth

Take my breath away
Take my breath away
Take my breath away

Take me

I AWAKEN

To my love
Gazing into my eyes
My reflection
In fathomless obsidian
Deeper
Than the deepest darkling
Of the Marianas
She whispers my name

I want to be
Intrepid
I want to be
Fearless
I want to be Hers

I am
Hers

SHE STANDS

Toes curled
Over the brink
Of a precipice
At the end of the land
On the edge of the world.

Hair whipped by wind
Chest forward
Eyes closed
Arms spread wide
As if to say, "Take me."

So abused
So damn broken
The brittle soul
Cracuelure du jour
Yet she is stronger than the strongest man.

So precisely balanced
Between land and sky
The weight of a mote
From the eye of a swallow
Could pitch her over.

Land.
Sky.
Solid.
Oblivion.

If I touch her
Over the side.

If I whisper in her ear, "Don't jump."
Over the side.

If I breathe; if my heart beats
Over the side.

She will fall
It is inevitable.
The only two questions
Are "When?"
And "Which way?"

Land.
Sky.
Solid.
Oblivion.
Land.
Sky.
Solid.
Oblivion.

In my life
The hardest thing I have ever done
Is nothing.

AND SO IT GOES

A lot of men have told me the same
things," she said, "as you have."

"Yes," I said, "but none of them
were me."

And so it goes.

She will believe me
Or she will not.

I am unaccustomed
To hope. My heart
is as still as a field mouse
in the presence of a murder
of crows.

CUCKOLD

She sleeps
With death
And incest
And pestilence
Seductive lies
The churning warmth
Of rot.

How can I possibly
Compete
With that?

MUTUALLY ASSURED DESTRUCTION

The only way
You could have betrayed me
Was to betray
Yourself.

HAIKU #2

How can I help you
When you're an accessory
In your own murder?

PROCESS OF ELIMINATION

It happens
No warning
Crack
Howling grinding
agony.

Days pass
The rage gives way
The pain falters
A dull throb
Between the ears.

It makes no sense
He loves me
I know this
He knew
How much this would hurt.

Maddening
A leaking faucet
A rock in a shoe
A crooked painting on the wall
An itch that cannot be

scratched.

Why?
Why?
Why?
Why?
Why?

The answer evades her
She need only ask him
But dares not
Because it is
The truth.

So she haunts him
Clings to him.
Don't let me go, she says.
Let me go, she says.
Please don't let me go, she says.

And he will speak her name
Thrice plus once
And she will know
Why And she will
No longer Be afraid.

MICHAEL

In a restroom at the Citgo on 14th and Central,
he leans on two palms planted
on the corners
of a sink patined with grime
and ancient soap scum. His flesh
is bruised and torn. His wings,
folded behind him, spattered
with filth, the feathers gray
and sopping, bent, broken
and disheveled.

He gazes into a cracked
mirror, nose bloody,
lip split and swollen,
punch-drunk eyes
as blue and ancient as the Mediterranean.
And he mutters,
"What the fuck was that all about?"

YOU KNOW WHAT YOU ARE

You puff your chest
And hold your weak chin high
Unswaying in your conviction
That you are the smartest one
In every room.
And how could that not be true
When you are so facile
At besting your betters?
But you know the truth,
Don't you?
The trick is in identifying
The weakness you will exploit
The almost imperceptible limp
The infection
The oozing wound
That defies healing.
True, your prey is better than you
(as are all creatures)
Save that flaw
That tragically fatal flaw.
That foolish longing to be cherished
To be respected
And protected

By another
You are a coward
Your victories are ash in your mouth
Your triumphs, hollow and preordained.
The fix is always in.
You cling to the carcass of your failure
Rend and ravage and rape it
Seeking, always seeking
The light that you obliterated.
You whine and keen
You drink
You rage

These pretty things
These pretty, pretty things
Lies!
All lies!
Time to move on
To the next
Lucky girl.

SHE CREATED

A vision
Of everything she wanted
To be.
A glorious thing
Strong and true.

It grew within her
Barren womb
Her only
Most beloved
Progeny.

What a fine child
It would have been
Had it not
Been strangled
By its own umbilical cord.

Still it is loved.
It is remembered.
Which is far far better
Than having never been
Anything.

DANIEL KNAUF

I rattle the bones
If only
To break
The terrible
Silence.

MY BED

Absent of you
A 35 square foot,
Barren,
Linen-wrapped plateau
Upon which I lay
Creased brown face up
Arms and legs splayed
Like a man dying
Of thirst,
Fingers curled
Nails dirty
Sightless eyes
Baked to eggwhites
By a pitiless sun.

I inhale and
I exhale.

BLEEDING

Profusely
From a dozen fatal wounds.
She clenches my hand
hard enough to grind bones.

She grins
a Colgate smile
smeared with crimson
and snarls, "What the fuck are you crying about?"

THIS IS THE HOUSE

That we built
A house with four bedrooms
Hot and cold running hearts
A view to die for
Vaulted dreams
Wall-to-wall disappointment
Such a fine design
Betrayed by a tragic
Execution.

NOHO GLOAMING

The ruthless burning orb dips
below the ragged ass-crack of Shaitan.
In the jacuzzi, dog-league rappers giggle
the theme from Jaws
as they stalk a tatted ginger
snowball.

I tip back a double
Single malt; neat. Hmm. Something nefarious
happening below the bubbles,
Ginger cranes her neck,
the back of her skull kissing
the deck; an opiated eyeroll,
baby-lips part
in a guttural moan. Our gazes meet;
lock. In that moment,
she shows me her terror
and I acknowledge it with a
sage nod; a silent good-luck-with-that.

It is the most I can
reasonably offer. She knows this.

But still,
she despises me.

IN THE YARD

I sit with my head between my knees
A drop of sweat tracking dust
Trickling down
The side of my nose.
Dangling off the tip.
Aware of the eyes
All those eyes!
Burning into me
Expectant
Embittered
Enraged
Envious
Because I have escaped
The balls
The chains
The bars
The locks
The shackles
That even now abrade
The skin on their wrists

They gaze at me
From cells

Each self-constructed from blocks
Of their flesh
Mortared and caulked
With their blood.

They scowl
At me
As I scowl
At the woman pirouetting
Outside
The electric fence I built.

She smiles like a Cheshire Cat

I rise.
I saunter toward her.
The trolls in the towers
Train their weapons
As I approach
The dead line.

I never
Ever
Look back.

SHE WAITS

In her favorite wingback chair
Her beloved dog curled in her lap
For the cavalry to come
And rescue her.

The bitter cold wind of yet another winter passing
Brushes her hair

A man stands behind her
His palm on her shoulder
A gesture of fondness
Were it not for the vise-grip

The bitter cold wind of yet another winter passing
Brushes her hair

And the dog is puzzled
Because the cavalry already came and went
Trumpets blowing
Banners flowing

Yet still she waits
For their arrival

And for each year past,
He takes ten
And for each of his dreams realized
A thousand of hers are Stillborn.

THE REAL PROBLEM

Isn't that I would have given you
Everything.
But that you would have
Taken it.

DEATH RATTLE

The banal paradigm cracks and
We glimpse the
Sublime, beautiful light
Behind it
And realize
Its terrible import

The collision of ecstasy and
Terror
That millisecond
Perfectly balanced
On the razor's edge
Between existence
And existence.

THE MOON

Captivated
Enchanted
Bathing in her cold cold light.
An illusion
Of illumination
Its source:

Whoever gazes upon her.

F-SHARP MINOR

Though you seemed intriguing
And your presence made for an entertaining first movement
It became repetitive
And increasingly tedious
In the second.

Well before the halfway point
It was abundantly clear
That you were, in fact, one note
Masquerading
As a chord.

The symphony is much stronger
Now that you are gone.

PRINCE CHARMING

He thought
The way to make
A woman cherish him
Was to spare no effort
Expense
Or sacrifice
To grant her heart's every desire.

After much anguish
And many crushing failures
He finally learned
That all he need do
Is give her
His undivided attention.

THE GIDDY THRILL

Experienced the first time one recognizes
One's own hopes, dreams and suffering
Residing in another
Is the very definition of The Ecstasy
Of Recognition
And when it is encountered
One is forever wiser

I pray you recognize
And draw wisdom
From my present
Agony

I love you
I love you
I love you
Goodbye.

HAPPILY EVER AFTER

Only in movies,
Insignificant novels,
And fairy tales.
In real life
There are happy moments
But never
Ever
Happy endings.
No exceptions.
I can still smell her;
Taste her;
Feel her.
I can still hear her sing along with the radio.
It echoes in my empty room.
Her impression in my bed,
Sheets long cold.
The ghost of us
Haunts me.
But I can still feel her
Like a phantom limb.

I hope.
I dream.

I pray for a happy ending.
God laughs,
That savage bastard,
Happily ever after,
Forever and ever,
Amen.

THIS ONE

Hot in the room
Stinking of self-deception
I awaken to the rhythmic hiss of rain
Pouring in sheets
Dripping clinking, clanking
Down roof gutters and pipes
The compulsion is irresistible
It is 3:10 AM by my phone
And the madness feels calm and sane

I pad downstairs
Collect what I need
Soap and two brand new fluffy white towels
Of virgin cotton
Tags still stapled from Bed, Bath
And Beyond

I lay one towel on the hardwood floor
Drape the other
Over the bannister of the landing
And step out the door
Onto my rooftop terrace
Fat cleansing drops from the heavens

Fall in sweeping sheets
Against the macadam
Forty feet below me
They whisper

This one
This one
This one
This one

As the piss-warm rain sluices down
My shoulders
My chest
My back
My belly
The wind mild but bracing
I soap up
A thousand dead gods
Chanting

This one
This one
This one
This one

Below the chorus
The thunder of the ocean
The roar of a departing 747
The clink clank clunk of the rain in the gutters
The Saltillo tiles treacherous
Under my bare feet
As that one is swept away
By time and distance and

This one
This one
This one
This one

I smile like an idiot
For the boon of crackling wisdom
The rain has gifted me
As that one
Is obliterated
Finally and forever by
This one
This one
This one
This one

And the millstone
Of being
Too good to be true
Falls away
And I kick free
Swimming
Ascending toward the quivering light
I breach the undulating surface
Reborn
Laughing
Breathing

This one
This one
This one
This one

And the world is her eyes
A sparkling, mysterious universe
Of dark matter
Dreams
And infinite possibilities
And the voices
Of a legion of angels
Whisper across the asphalt
Insistent

In windy sheets

This one
This one
This one
This one

Joined by a single smoky voice
Her voice
Rising like a memory
Of a celestial aria
I have yet to hear
"I don't need you to be
Too good to be true

Just be

True."

TRUE LOVE

A sirocco
Hollow as an empty tomb
Filled with the shrieks of every human
Who has suffered
Wrenching loss.
Carves the earth
Serpentine madhouse gouges
Obliterating one house
Leaving its neighbor standing
Untouched.

Skies bleed
Lightning flashes
Green and purple and crimson.

The sane
Huddle in basements
Muttering prayers
To a capricious God.
The mad
Wander the streets
Giggling and weeping
These words muttered

With the giddy thrill
Of tightrope walkers
Traversing the abyss:

"I love you."
"I love you, too."

PERFECTION

Outside Kyoto
The old man in the moss garden
Takes great care
Not to rake up
Every single
Umber
Gold
Autumn leaf

In the heart of Rome
At the Hotel Locarno
There is a hole in the roof
Above the passage
From the bar
To the patio
Where the rain gets in
Which will never be repaired

Below the left eye
Of my love
There is a fine lacework
Of filigreed lines

Scrolled by 1,000 smiles
I kiss her
There.

606

In the ever sprawling
Rambling mansion
There is a room
Papered in scarlet damask
Its twelve foot ceiling
Wreathed in deeply carved
White lacquered
Crown moulding
A crystal chandelier
Mahogany floors
A single
Large window

Cold light drills though
Illuminating an unmade bed.
The twisted sheets remember

We were there

You were there

I was there

NOHO GLOAMING

Now we are apart

Together.

QUEUE

As the line ahead grows ever shorter
You turn and hundreds stand
Behind you
And you feel a smug satisfaction in this
Entirely unwarranted
Because it is inevitable
If one stands in line
Long enough

We suffer
We are cold
We weep
Wounds are inflicted
Most heal
Some not

And still
The longer you wait
You cannot help
But become
Increasingly aware
Of each moment
Each kind word

Each lingering gaze
Each gentle caress
Each tear of rapture

To learn
To savor these
Moments
Is to be
Wise

THIS FINE THING

Stir
Open my eyes
Look around
A gray ghost of the promised dawn
Paints one wall
A broad diagonal stripe
Turning the color
Of a ripe peach
As the promise is fulfilled
I turn

And see you sleeping
And I whisper
Anything could happen today
My love
Anything
Is that not

Wonderful?

THE CURIOUS CODA OF ANTHONY SANTOS

Anthony Santos
(formerly known as "Tony Shoulders"),
relaxes in his genuine Eames Chair,
in his authentic mid-century modern
Post and beam.
Deep in the bone-dry cradle of the Mojave
Alone in the "Wonder Valley"
(AKA the "Neither Nor")

Alone.
Not another ranch for miles.
Sitting on as much land as the Witness Protection Program
Was stupid enough to give him
For testifying to everything
The Feds knew
All along.

(Yeah.)

(That Tony Shoulders.)

He hears a curiously soft, persistent
knocking

over the wind.

At first attributing it to
His genuine antique ceiling fan,
He shuts it off, and yet
The muted knocking persists.

A protracted
Intermittent
Pitter patter
Against the plate-glass
Of his floor-to-ceiling
Southwestern exposure.

And though Tony is curious
He cannot see outside,
For he had treated the windows
With professionally installed
Dark mahogany
plantation blinds.

And so,
Eyes locked on the closed shutters,
Tony picks up the remote
And presses: OPEN

With a tiny whine of cams and servos
The 4-inch shutters pivot open
And for a moment, so bizarre
Is the unfolding tableau outside
It is incomprehensible.
But as the slots inexorably widen
The truth of the horror beyond the glass
Ever so gradually
Reveals itself.

(Begging your pardon, ladies and gents;
but I feel it incumbent upon me

To inform you that,
Though I am drawing this out a bit
Consider it stylized.
The literary actualization of cinematic technique
Slow motion.
Perhaps a little bullet-time ramping.
Perhaps...

Nevertheless, to Tony,
the horrific reality
Of the nightmare diorama
Was immediate;
A flash.
A flourish.
Full blown.
A hideous epiphany.)

For piled four feet high outside
Pressed flat against his picture-windows
Are the wriggling, fluttering, squirming
Dying atop
The dead atop
The crushed atop
A molten base of ocher jelly.
And visible above
The twitching, crawling crust
Of what must have been a mountain of dead and dying insects,
Silhouetted against the gloaming,
A darkly mesmerizing tableau unfolds.

More moths. Thousands. Tens of thousands.
Hundreds of tens.
As large as swallows.
Wingspans perhaps seven inches tip-to-tip,
Thoraces thick as thimbles,
Fluttering then
Tucking their wings flat against their sides
Bold furry falcons

In a kamikaze dive
Tora...
Fucking TORA...
Fucking TORAAAAAHHHHHHH—

(thump)

As soft as an aborted child's first and only
Raging act of defiance:
A perfectly formed
But breathlessly small
Human hand
Curled into a fist.

(thump)

(thump... thump... tha-thump...)

Hypnotized, Tony approaches the glass
The angle of the rays cast by the dying sun
Magically
Rendering the mobster's chronically flaccid, jowly deadpan
Into the benevolent masque of a Tiki God
Happy and toothsome
Eyes sparkling with light refracted
Through the punctuation marks
Rendered in golden, jellied viscera.
On the glass.
Periods. Commas.
Exclamation points.

Then, he discerns
A subtle change in the key
Of the knocks.
(thump... tha-thump... tha-thump-pump...)
A gradual rise from F-flat to F-sharp.
And Tony's dim, piggy eyes begin
To ever so gradually

Widen
As he realizes
The effect of the growing pile—
The sheer, pressing, relentless
Mass of it;
The weight of it—
Against the glass
Brittle fusion
Stressing to the point
Of catastrophic failure
And...
And...
(thumpathump... thumpumpaththththumpumpump...)
And ohmyfuckingshitholyCHRIST!

BUT...

They could never get through
Those solid mahogany blinds!
And he's got enough bottled water
and MREs
Stockpiled in the panic-room
To hole up for six months
By himself.
Ride it out
Until the sickening soft, relentless pitter-patter
Slows
And ceases.

... if it ever slows.

... if it ever ceases.

For things as rare as an enraged swarm
Of moths the size of swallows
Have a habit of behaving
In unpredictable ways.

(Yes, Dear Reader, I did flog
the ever-living shit out of that horse's tired carcass.
But as I like to say, when mining a vein of inspiration,
good God,
eat the entire fucking buffalo!)

Tony snaps out of it
He squashes the button on the remote
Jabs it with his big fat thumb.
And tragically betrayed
By what his fancy doctors call
Essential palmar hyperhidrosis
("sweaty palms" between you and me)
The cricket-sized lozenge of a remote
Is ejected by the pressure
Of fleshy finger-pads
Devoid of whorls and ridges
(For long ago
Tony had his fingerprints dissolved with acid.)
Smooth and pink
And slick due to essential palmar hyperhidrosis, of course!
(of course...)
(oh yes...)
(and...)
(thumpathumpumpumpaththththumpumpump)
FUCK!!!

The lozenge propelled
Clear across the room,
Caroming off the "vintage" HiFi (Sony guts!)
Skittering across the mirror-polished bamboo floor.

(And that's good, right? he thinks, That's good for the environ-
ment! Sustainable. Because say what you will about Tony Shoul-
ders, I am environmentally responsible to a fucking tee! And if I
do that one good thing, it makes me a good person? Right? Say
amen-alleluia! Alleluia! That makes me a righteous person!
Right? Say Praise The Lord! Praise the LORD! That makes me a

69

righteous and capricious little god, because I, Tony Shoulders,
am created in My Maker's Image!)

And, in the best inner-voice impersonation of Charlton
Heston Tony can muster,
He bellows,
"And I shall cast the shrieking souls
of the cruelly insensitive
The shockingly unhorrified,
And ever-so-unevolved,
And ever-so-common,
Background players.
Extras!
Each and every one!
Into the river
of boiling murderer's blood
Coursing through Dante's Seventh Circle
Called The Phlegethon.

The remote
Skitters across the floor and under
his authentic vintage '50s Danish modern sofa.
And he spins,
realizing from the sudden cessation
Of the whir of servos,
that the button he jabbed
with his scarred-slick-sweaty fat thumb
was not CLOSE...

... but STOP.

Tony did the math:
In seconds, those windows are gonna implode.
He could hear faint crackling with each soft impact.
He had two choices:

1.) Run through that door, left down the hall, through the hidden
panel

Into the Panic Room
Slam and bolt the hermetically sealed door.
Imprisoned in a 50 foot square galvanized box,
Listening to the news on his wind-up radio
Devastating swarms
As vast and thick as cumulus clouds
Gray-brown-black
And ragged about the edges.
Swirling
Whispering
Descending
Smothering
Los Angeles
New York
London
Sao Paulo
Mambasa
St. Petersburg
Constantinople
Vatican City
Like a dirge
To the accompaniment
Of a Gene Krupa solo
Played with rolled silk napkins
(thump... thump-thump-tha-pump...)
In that box
For six months
And then...?

Fucking starve to death...?

Fuck that!

So he considers:

2.) Leap over that reproduction Noguchi coffee-table;
(Yeah, reproduction. So what? Why bother.
The things are so fucking obsequious these days!)

grab that remote;
spring-roll it like Jackie Chan;
leap up;
drop into a crouch.
Aim the lozenge
O.G. Star Trek mini-phaser-style.
And cooly press: CLOSE

And Tony will not only have the panic room; He'll have the run
of the whole place! The booze, the Omaha steaks, the smut, the
jacuzzi tub, the sauna...

Of course, he leaps.

Of course.

Alas, there is no Jackie Chan spring-roll.

The problem is not a lack of momentum
But an absence of lift.
Hurtling, lumbering forward
Tony barks both kneecaps
Into bloody meal
Against the edge of the 1-inch thick
Glass tabletop.
He pitches violently forward
Open satin kimono fluttering back
Like the vestigial wings
Of a bloated, flightless bird
His naked, round, sweaty belly
SMACKING the flat surface of the glass
With shattering force!
Shattering!
Yet, miraculously, it doesn't!
Had it,
Tony's big gut would have been
slashed, sliced, stabbed by the shards
And he no doubt would have bled out instantly.

But as it is, he scored bonus-time!
Delaying his demise a full 12 seconds!

The tabletop and Tony
Slides
Belly down
Eyes forward
Onto the mirror polished bamboo floor Gliding...
No! Hydro-planing!
On a thin layer
Of oleaginous
Belly-sweat.
Immediately hitting mad speed
And rocketing across that floor
Past the keys
Under the tall teak legs of the sofa
Abruptly jerking to a stop
Impeded by his gargantuan ass!
And, grunting, he laboriously pulls himself free;
Twists around,
Gazing up at the windows
Safety-glass fogged by millions of micro-fractures,
Billowing in
Bulging to a stiff, steady gust
Like the black sails on a pirate's galleon.

And as Tony watches, eyes agog with terror,
The membranous film
Sandwiched between the two thin sheets of tempered glass
Fails

And the whispering swarm avalanches on Tony.
He gasps aloud: "Musta been... one of them... government
experiments-gone-wrong,"
The words accompanied by the thrilling surge
of an aggrieved citizen's righteous indignation
Before succumbing to choking
Gasping, blind, protracted strangulation

Fluttering
Whispering
Fluttering
Words soft, spoken by
A hundred-million wings:
"12 more fucking seconds"
The whirring flutter whispers
"12 more fucking seconds"
Choking crawling squirming probing fluttering...
"12 more fucking seconds"
"12 more fucking seconds"
"12 more fucking seconds"
The fluttering
The flicking of countless paper wings
Clustering
Invading his mouth like an angry mob
Rampaging down his throat
Smothering
Smothering
12... more... fucking seconds!

Gray...

Brown...

Black...

12 seconds...

20 seconds...

1 minute...

3 minutes...

(fluttering)

6 minutes and 37 seconds

Of grindingly slow

Asphyxiation.

And in the humid darkness
Steeped in a foul stench of fear and decay
Tony hears the anguished shrieks
of a billion damned souls
And he discerns
the rapidly approaching,
Sinuously undulating,
Bubbling steaming stinking
Ruby-red surface
of The Phlegethon

ABOUT THE AUTHOR

Daniel Knauf created and served as executive producer and writer of his Emmy Award-winning series *Carnivàle* (HBO)., He subsequently wrote and produced a number of television series, including *Supernatural* (The CW), *Fear Itself* (NBC) and *Spartacus: Blood and Sand* (Starz). Most recently, he served as the showrunner and executive producer-writer of the NBC series *Dracula* and as a writer-Executive Producer on the NBC TV's hit primetime drama *The Blacklist* starring James Spader. In the comics arena, Mr. Knauf and his son Charles Knauf collaborated on *The Invincible Iron Man, Captain America*, and *The Eternals* for Marvel as well as the SyFy pilot/mini, *The Phantom*. In features,

Mr. Knauf has developed an epic vampire trilogy, *The House of Cain*, for Will Smith and Overbrook Productions. Daniel is also the CEO of Bxx, LLC, a studio specializing in transmedia and box narratives.

NoHo Gloaming is his first published collection of poetry.

ALSO BY CLASH BOOKS

TRAGEDY QUEENS: STORIES INSPIRED BY LANA DEL REY & SYLVIA PLATH

edited by Leza Cantoral

DARK MOONS RISING IN A STARLESS NIGHT

Mame Bougouma Diene

NOHO GLOAMING & THE CURIOUS CODA OF ANTHONY SANTOS

Daniel Knauf (Creator of HBO's Carnivàle)

IF YOU DIED TOMORROW I WOULD EAT YOUR CORPSE

Wrath James White

GIRL LIKE A BOMB

Autumn Christian

THE ANARCHIST KOSHER COOKBOOK

Maxwell Bauman

HORROR FILM POEMS

Christoph Paul

NIGHTMARES IN ECTASY

Brendan Vidito

THE VERY INEFFECTIVE HAUNTED HOUSE

Jeff Burk

Printed in the USA
CPSIA information can be obtained
at www.ICGtesting.com
JSHW080005150824
68134JS00021B/2283